CARBON in the GARDEN

ORGANIC TIPS FOR A SUSTAINABLE GARDEN AND PLANET

Emily Morris   **Nathaniel Morris**

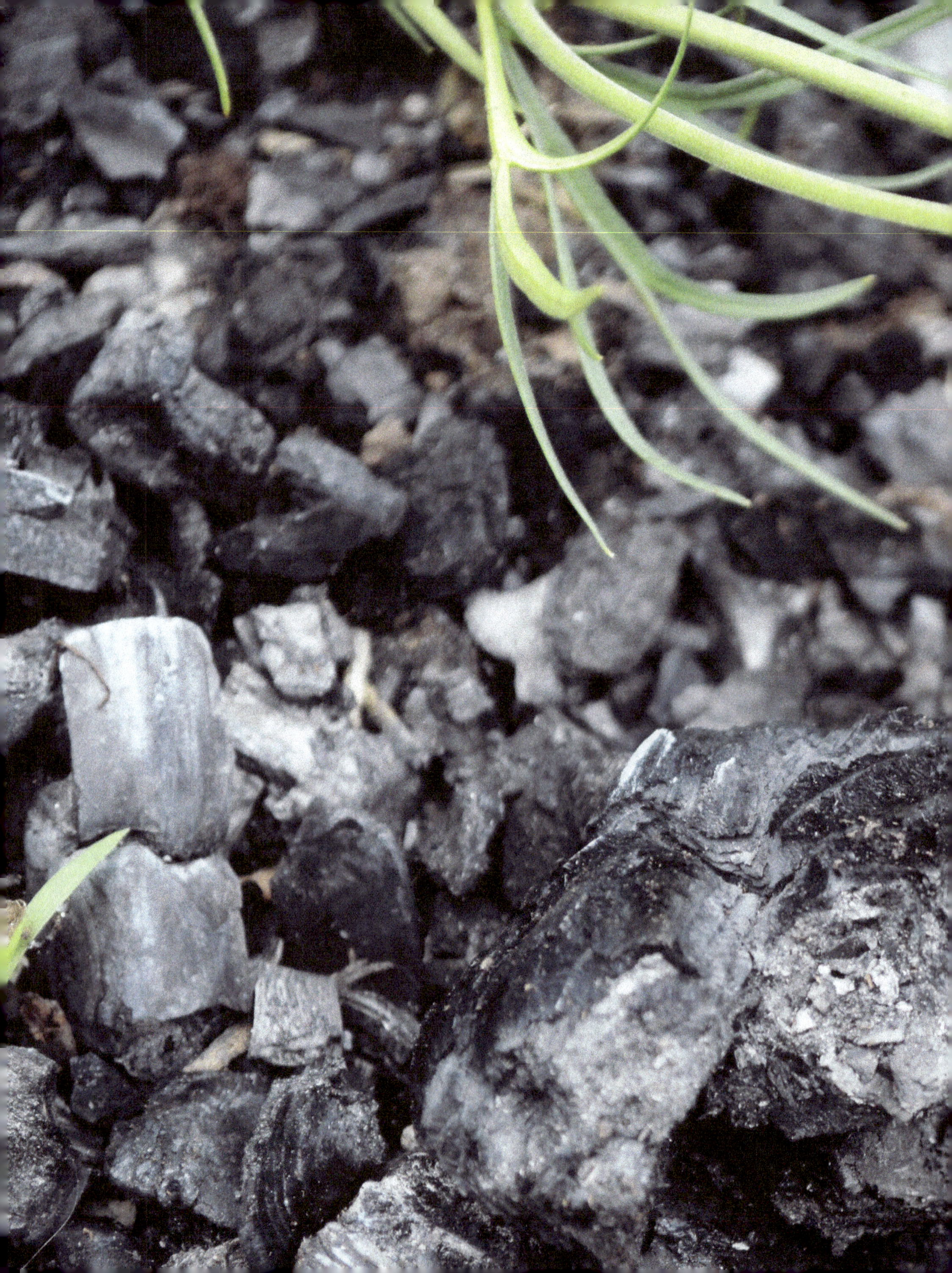

Content produced in Smiths Falls, Ontario

ISBN #
978-1-7782976-4-9 E-book
978-1-7782976-3-2 Paperback
978-1-7782976-5-6 Hardcover

LEGAL DISCLAIMER

Carbon in the Garden by Nathaniel Morris and Emily Morris is intended for informational purposes only. The authors, publisher, and distributors of this book make no representations or warranties regarding the suitability, accuracy, or safety of the information contained within these pages. It is essential that you consult with relevant fire authorities for guidance and permission before attempting to make biochar.

Dangers Associated with Creating High-Temperature Fires for Biochar Production:
The production of biochar involves the creation of high-temperature fires, which can be inherently dangerous. These risks include, but are not limited to:

Fire Hazards: High-temperature fires can pose a risk of uncontrolled fires, resulting in property damage, injury, or loss of life. It is essential to follow all safety precautions, local laws, and regulations regarding fire safety when producing biochar.

Health Hazards: Exposure to smoke and harmful gases produced during the biochar production process can lead to respiratory issues and other health concerns. It is crucial to wear appropriate protective gear and operate in well-ventilated areas to minimize risks.

The information provided in this book is meant to be a starting point for your research and should not be considered a comprehensive guide. By using this book, you agree to assume all risks associated with making and using biochar and release the authors, publisher, and distributors from any liability for any injury, loss, damage, or harm that may result from your use of the information contained herein.

Readers are encouraged to conduct thorough research, seek expert advice, and use their best judgment when engaging in biochar production and use, while always prioritizing safety, responsibility, and compliance with the law.

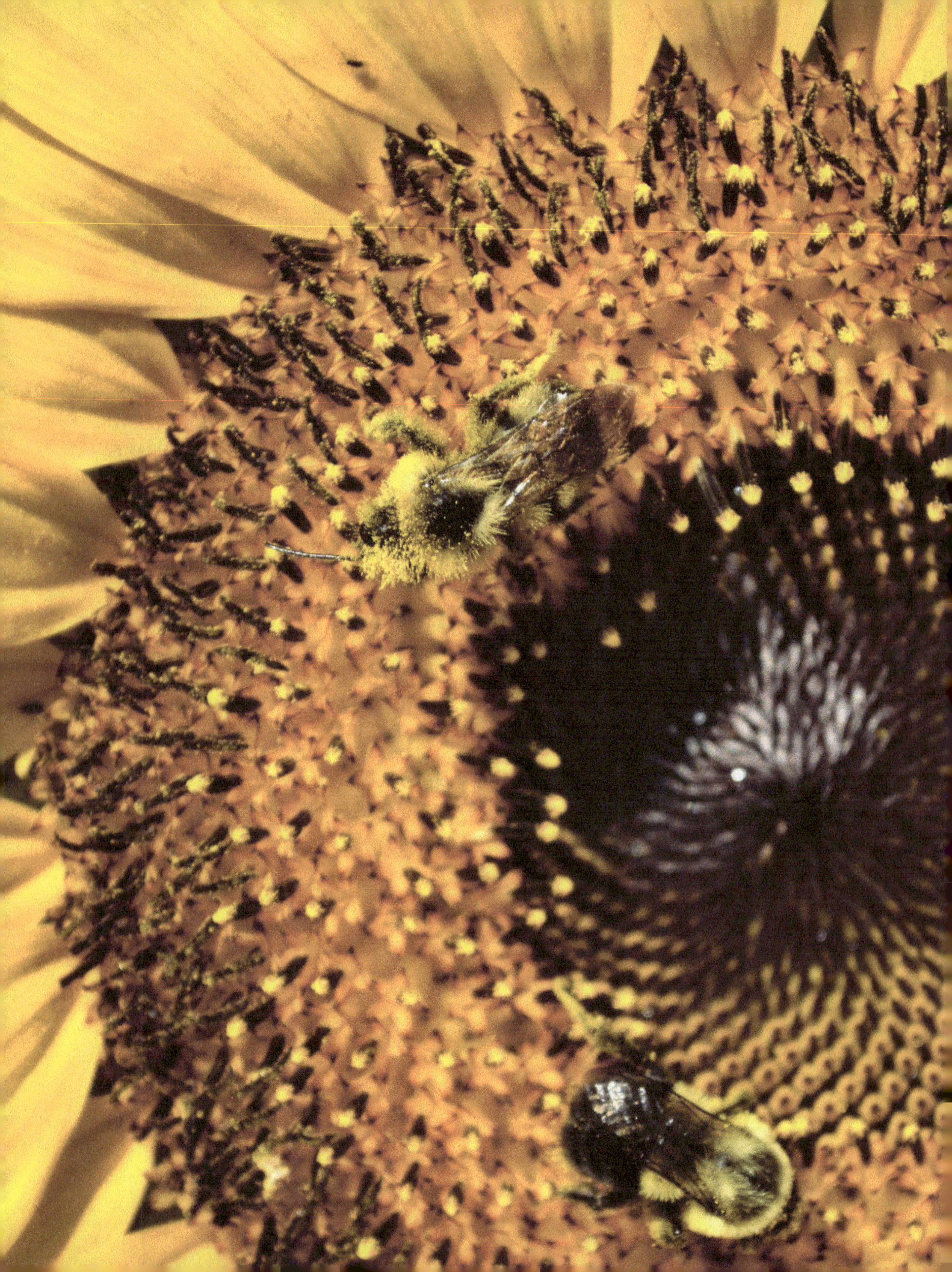

Introduction

In the quest to combat climate change, there is a powerful weapon in our arsenal that has stood the test of time, rooted in the wisdom of the Amazonian aboriginal people.

Welcome to *Carbon in the Garden*, a guide that illuminates the remarkable efficacy of biochar production and its role as one of the most efficient ways to fight climate change.

Deep within the dense expanse of the Amazon rainforest lies a testament to the resilience and ingenuity of indigenous civilizations: terra preta, the legendary dark earth. For over a millennium, the Amazonian aboriginal people harnessed the power of biochar to create this fertile soil, demonstrating its long-term safety and effectiveness at scale. Today, we have the opportunity to embrace their legacy and channel their wisdom into a global movement for climate restoration.

Carbon in the Garden embarks on an exploration of the immense potential of biochar production as a climate change mitigation strategy. This approach centers on the sustainable cultivation of biomass, which is then converted into **biochar** through a process called pyrolysis.

Biochar is a highly stable form of carbon-rich charcoal that can be incorporated into soils, locking away carbon for centuries and promoting soil health simultaneously.

What sets biochar apart is its extraordinary efficiency in addressing climate change. Dollar for dollar, it is one of the most impactful and cost-effective strategies available. By sequestering carbon in biochar and incorporating it into agricultural systems, we can reduce greenhouse gas emissions while simultaneously enhancing soil fertility, improving water retention, and boosting crop yields.

This powerful symbiosis ensures that every investment in biochar yields multiple benefits, making it a compelling choice for individuals, communities, and policymakers seeking to make a tangible difference.

Crucially, the Amazonians have gifted us with more than just a time-tested technique. They have provided a blueprint for assessing the safety and scalability of climate solutions. While we cannot predict the future or dismiss the possibility of new technologies emerging, we must prioritize the assurance of safety. Biochar, with its millennia-old track record, offers us a critical standard against which we can measure and evaluate the safety of hypothetical alternatives. It serves as a beacon, reminding us to approach new technologies with caution and rigorous scrutiny, ensuring that they too can demonstrate their long-term safety and efficacy.

Carbon in the Garden takes a journey that merges ancient wisdom with modern science and innovation. By embracing the power of biochar, we tap into the vast potential for transforming our agricultural systems and revitalizing our planet. This guide is an impassioned call to action, urging individuals and communities to adopt this proven strategy and weave it into the fabric of their lives.

Together, we have the opportunity to rekindle our connection with the earth, restoring balance, and securing a sustainable future. As we explore the remarkable efficiency and safety of biochar, we embrace the notion that biochar serves not only as a vital solution in its own right but also as a touchstone for assessing the safety of future technologies. Join us in cultivating carbon in the garden, and let us forge a path toward a resilient, carbon-negative future for generations to come.

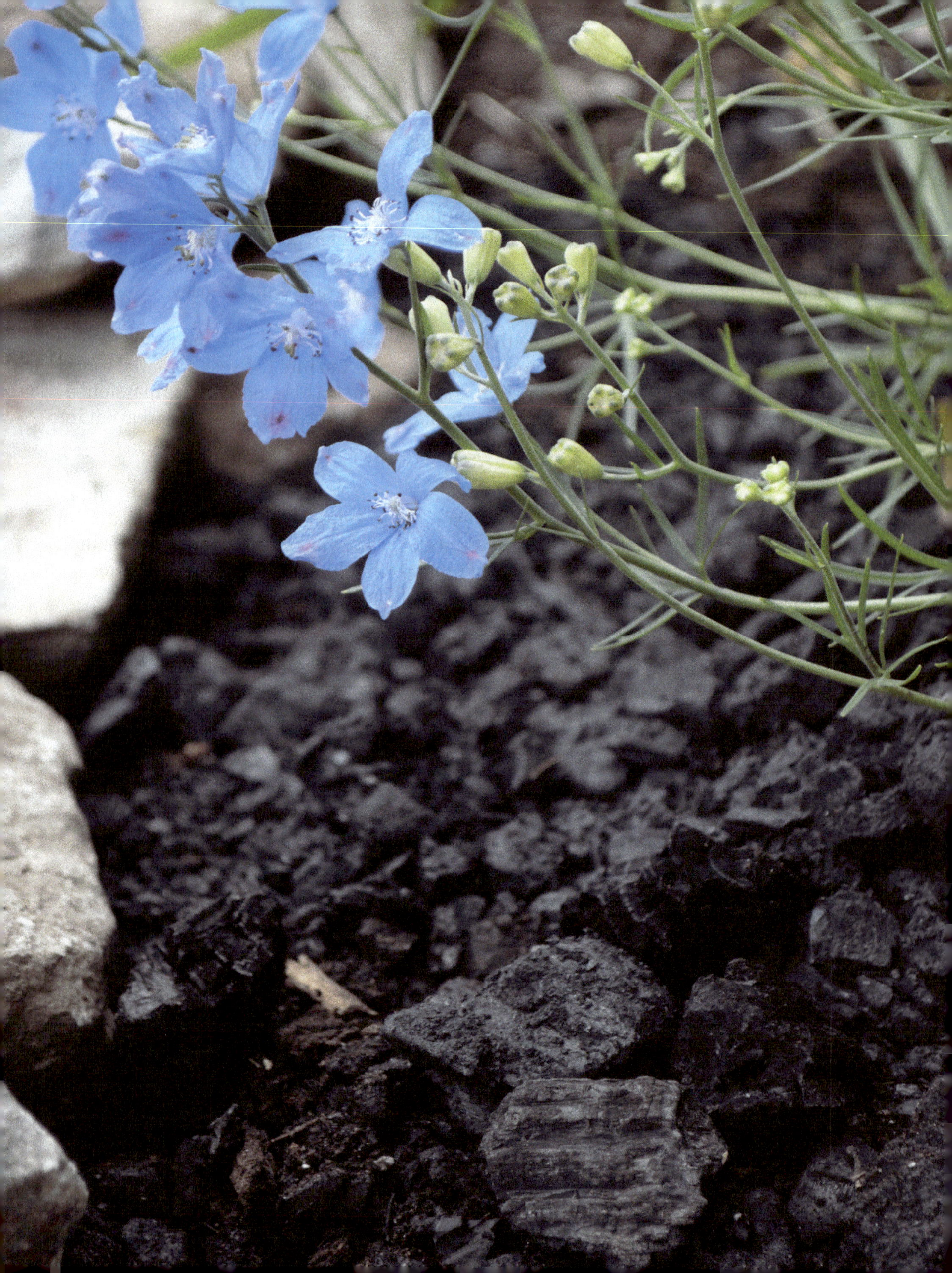

Chapter 1

What is Biochar?

Introduction to Biochar

In our journey to understand the power and potential of biochar, we must first unravel the fundamental aspects of this remarkable substance. Biochar is a form of carbon-rich charcoal produced through a process known as pyrolysis.

This ancient technique of transforming biomass into a stable and beneficial carbon product has been practiced for millennia, notably by the indigenous peoples of the Amazon rainforest. In this chapter, we delve into the intricacies of pyrolysis and explore the cone pit method, a time-honored approach to biochar production employed by the Amazonians.

WHAT IS BIOCHAR?

Biochar is pure carbon made by a process known as pyrolysis using high temperatures in a low-oxygen environment. Biochar is great as a tool in organic gardening because it is very porous and attracts plant foods like a magnet. It can hold water, nutrients, and microorganisms, making it an optimal habitat for beneficial soil microbes that help plants grow.

ADDING BIOCHAR TO YOUR SOIL CAN:

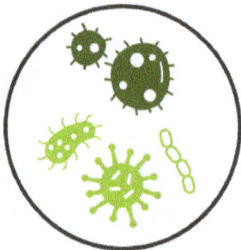

+
INCREASE MICROBIAL ACTIVITY & DIVERSITY

+
INCREASE WATER RETENTION

+
INCREASE CATION EXCHANGE CAPACITY (CEC)

BIOCHAR Is produced using biomass through the process of pyrolysis

Biochar can improve soil fertility & sequester carbon

PYROLYSIS
PROCESS OF PRODUCING BIOCHAR

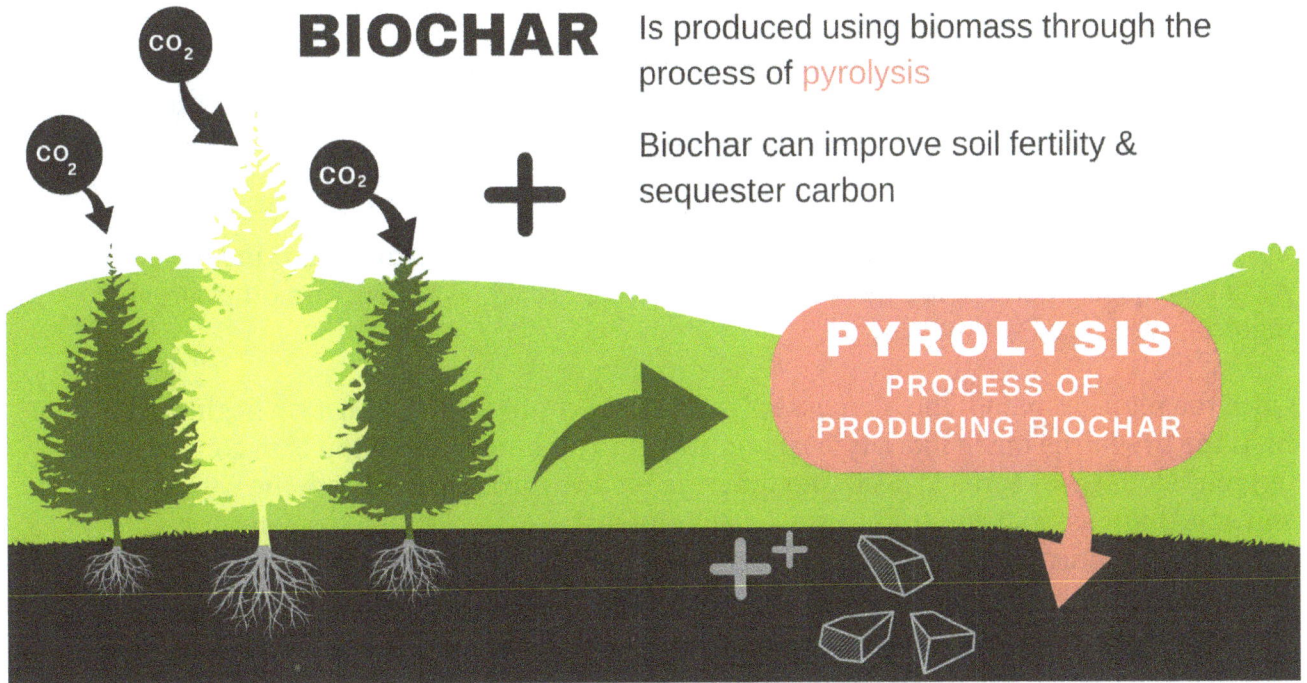

Pyrolysis: The Art of Transforming Biomass

At the heart of biochar production lies the transformative process of pyrolysis. Pyrolysis involves heating biomass, such as plant residues or agricultural waste, in the absence of oxygen. This controlled thermal decomposition leads to the release of volatile gases and liquids, leaving behind a carbonaceous residue known as biochar.

The key to successful pyrolysis lies in carefully managing the temperature and oxygen levels during the process. By ensuring limited oxygen availability, a crucial chemical reaction called gasification occurs. During gasification, the volatile components of the biomass break down into gasses such as methane, carbon monoxide, and hydrogen. The remaining solid residue, which retains a high proportion of carbon, is the biochar we seek.

PYROLISIS = Heating biomass in a **HIGH TEMP** ⬆ **LOW OXYGEN** ⬇ environment to harden carbon in place

The Cone Pit Method: A Time-Honored Tradition

One of the earliest methods of biochar production is the cone pit method, which was mastered by the Amazonian aboriginal people. This technique harmonizes with the surrounding environment, utilizing readily available biomass and minimizing the impact on the ecosystem.

The cone pit method involves creating a carefully constructed pit in the ground. A cone-shaped mound of biomass, consisting of plant residues, wood, and other organic materials, is placed within the pit.

Once the pit is prepared, the biomass is ignited, and controlled combustion begins. At first, the fire burns much like a typical bonfire, as the biomass at the top is in contact with oxygen. As the heat spreads deep into the cone pit away from the oxygen, the wood gases leave the biomass and combust as they reach the surface. The limited oxygen supply within the pit encourages pyrolysis, thereby maximizing biochar production. The process can take several hours, depending on the size of the pit and the desired outcome.

A Step-by-Step Guide:

MAKING BIOCHAR WITH THE CONE PIT METHOD

Materials You Will Need:

1.
SHOVEL OR DIGGING TOOLS

2.
ORGANIC BIOMASS
Wood chips, branches or logs

3.
FIRE SOURCE

4.
WATER SOURCE FOR SAFETY

5.
HOSE OR BUCKETS OF WATER

A Step-by-Step Guide:
MAKING BIOCHAR WITH THE CONE PIT METHOD

Step 1. Choose a Time & Location

Choosing an appropriate and safe burn site for a cone pit involves considering several factors:

Location

Select a location that is far away from any flammable structures, vegetation, or objects. Ideally, choose an open area in your yard or garden with good ventilation.

Clearance

Ensure a clear area around the pit, free from grass, leaves, or any other combustible materials. Remove any debris or dry vegetation from the vicinity.

Weather Conditions

Pay attention to weather conditions like droughts or extreme heat. Burning during dry spells can increase the risk of fires spreading.

Wind Conditions

Be mindful of wind direction and speed. Avoid burning on windy days, as gusts can spread embers and flames beyond the pit area and can also add too much oxygen for full pyrolysis to occur.

A Step-by-Step Guide:
MAKING BIOCHAR WITH THE CONE PIT METHOD

Terrain

Ensure the burn site is on stable ground to prevent the pit from collapsing while burning.

Local Regulations

Check local regulations and ordinances regarding open burning. Some areas may have restrictions or require permits for open fires.

Supervision

Always supervise the burn. Do not leave the fire unattended, especially during the ignition and burning phases.

Safety Equipment

Have firefighting equipment on hand, such as a hose or buckets of water, in case of emergencies. A fire extinguisher is also a good safety measure.

Children & Pets

Keep children and pets at a safe distance from the burn site to prevent accidents.

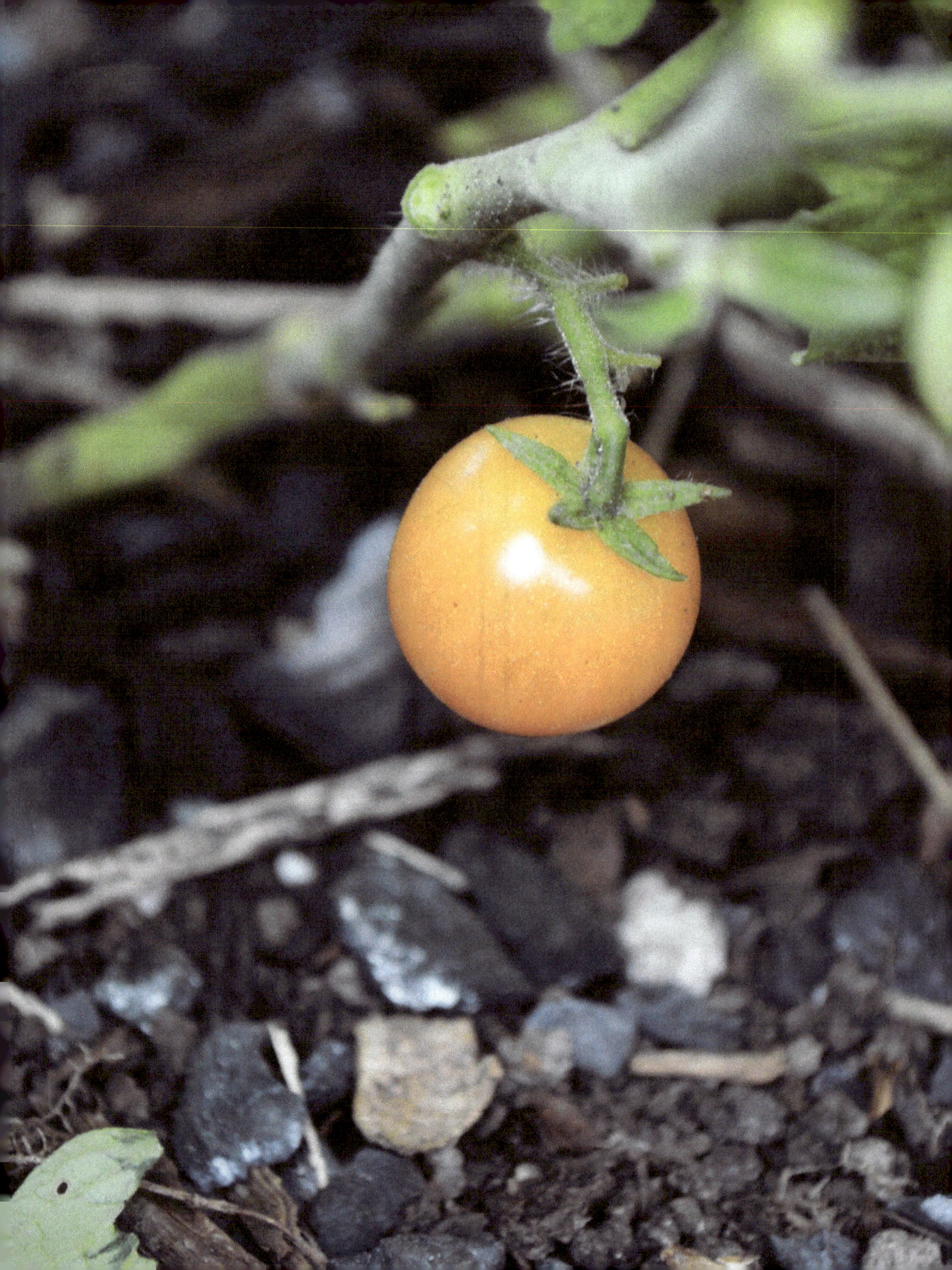

A Step-by-Step Guide:
MAKING BIOCHAR WITH THE CONE PIT METHOD

Step 2.   Dig the Cone Pit

Use a shovel or digging tools to dig a pit in the ground. The size of the pit will depend on the amount of biomass you have, but it should generally be about 2-3 feet in diameter and 2-3 feet deep.

Cone Pit

Step 3.   Gather Biomass

Collect the organic material, like branches, wood chips, and logs, you want to convert into biochar. Make sure the biomass is dry for better combustion.

MAKING BIOCHAR WITH THE CONE PIT METHOD

Step 4. ▼ Fill the Pit

Place the biomass inside the pit, stacking it in the shape of a cone. Then build another cone on top, just like you would for a camp fire. Leave an opening at the top to allow for air circulation and ignition.

▼ Biochar Cone Pit vs. Campfire

The bonfire on the right burns with lots of oxygen, leaving only ash. The pit fire on the left starts with oxygen on top but turns into a low-oxygen fire below, leaving charcoal instead of ash.

A Step-by-Step Guide:
MAKING BIOCHAR WITH THE CONE PIT METHOD

Step 5. 🔥   Ignite the Biomass

Use your fire source, matches or a lighter, to ignite the top of the biomass cone. Ensure that the fire catches and starts to burn.
The flames should be allowed to spread down into the pit.

A Step-by-Step Guide:
MAKING BIOCHAR WITH THE CONE PIT METHOD

Step 6. 👁 Monitor the Burn

Keep a close eye on the burn to ensure it continues evenly. You may need to add more biomass as it burns down to maintain the cone shape.

Step 7. 💧 Water Quench

Once the biomass has turned into glowing embers with minimal flame and you've achieved the desired amount of biochar, it's time to quench the fire.

Use a hose or buckets of water to thoroughly soak the biochar and extinguish any remaining embers. This step is essential for stopping the combustion process and cooling the biochar quickly.

A Step-by-Step Guide:
MAKING BIOCHAR WITH THE CONE PIT METHOD

Step 8. 😊 Uncover and Collect Biochar

After quenching, carefully remove the cover and inspect the biochar. It should be dark, brittle, and have a porous structure. Collect the biochar for the next phase where the biochar is charged with plant nutrients and inoculated with live beneficial fungi.

Chapter 2

The Bio in Biochar: Unveiling the Role of Mycorrhizal Fungi

Introduction to Mycorrhizal Fungi

In our exploration of the biochar microbiome, one group of microorganisms stands out for its extraordinary partnership with plants: mycorrhizal fungi. These fascinating fungi form symbiotic associations with plant roots, creating a mutually beneficial relationship that profoundly influences nutrient exchange, crop yield, and carbon sequestration.

In this chapter, we delve into the intricate mechanisms by which mycorrhizal fungi enhance plant nutrition, promote carbon sequestration, and contribute to sustainable agricultural practices.

ROOTS

ROOTS
+ MYCELIUM

RHIZOSPHERE

MYCORRHIZOSPHERE

Mycorrhizal fungi form a mutually beneficial relationship with plant roots, exchanging nutrients for carbohydrates, thereby extending the reach of the plant's rhizosphere to form a mycorrhizosphere. In doing this, the mycorrhizal fungi help take carbon that plants have pulled from the atmosphere and lock it into the soil. Best of all, mycorrhizal fungi can be cultivated on biochar!

When mycorrhizal fungi are grown on biochar, they colonize its porous structure, creating a "biochar-mycorrhizal complex". When this complex is added to soil, the biochar provides a stable substrate to supercharge the mycorrhizosphere, which further enhances the soil's ability to sequester carbon.

Nutrient Exchange and Enhanced Yield

Mycorrhizal fungi form a network of hyphae that extends beyond the reach of plant roots, exploring the soil and accessing nutrients that may be otherwise inaccessible to plants.

Through their intricate hyphal structures, these fungi effectively mine the soil, extracting nutrients such as phosphorus, nitrogen, and micronutrients. The fungi then transport these nutrients directly to the plant roots, facilitating their absorption and utilization by the plants.

In return for their nutrient provision, plants supply mycorrhizal fungi with a vital energy source: carbon in the form of sugars. Through photosynthesis, plants capture carbon dioxide from the atmosphere, converting it into sugars. A portion of these sugars is allocated to the mycorrhizal fungi, fueling their growth and sustenance. This exchange of nutrients and carbon establishes a powerful synergy, enhancing plant growth, increasing crop yield, and reducing the need for external fertilizers.

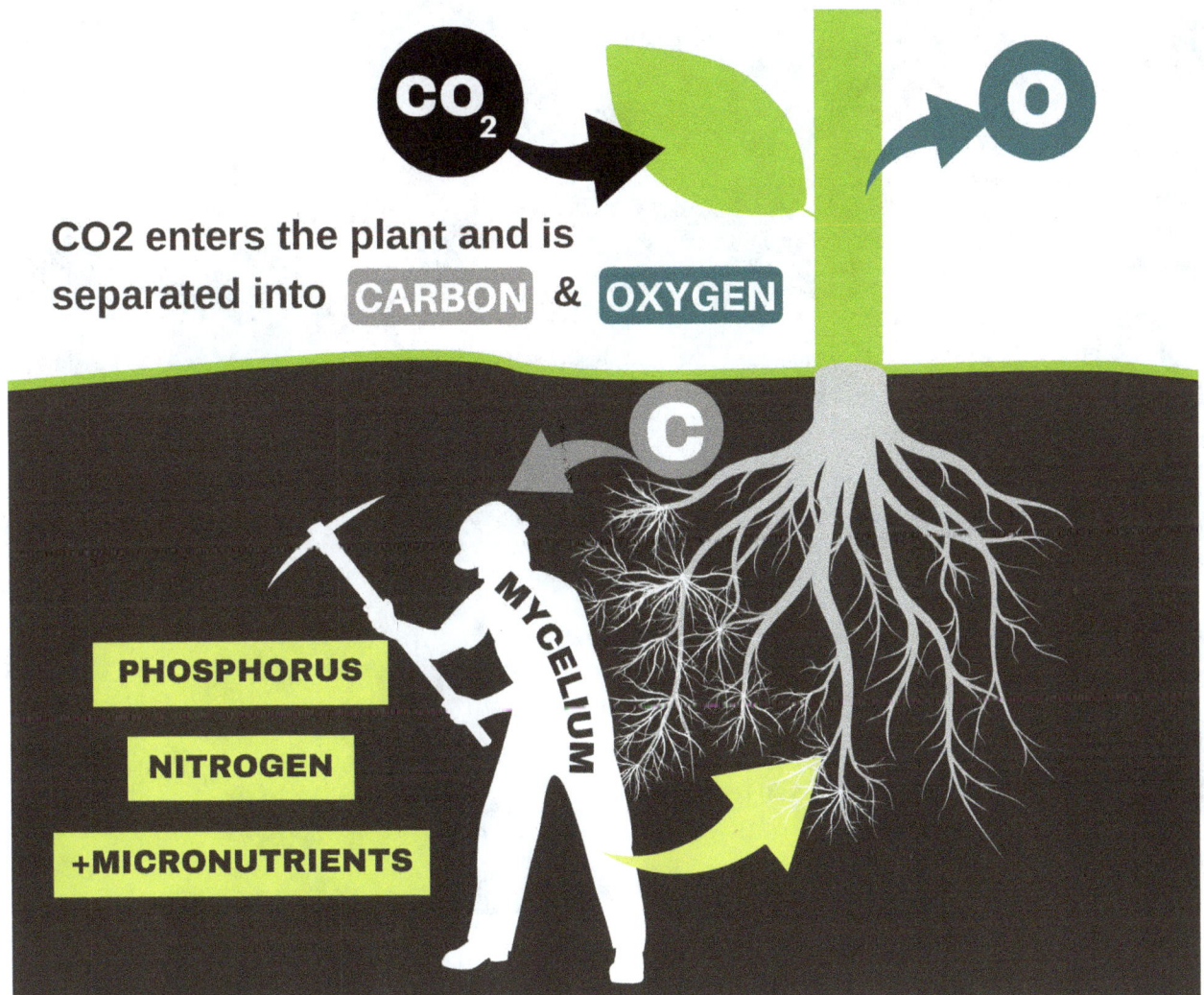

CO2 enters the plant and is separated into CARBON & OXYGEN

MYCELIUM

PHOSPHORUS

NITROGEN

+MICRONUTRIENTS

Carbon Sequestration and Soil Carbon Pool

The mycorrhizal symbiosis not only influences plant nutrition but also plays a significant role in the carbon cycle and soil carbon sequestration.

As plants assimilate atmospheric carbon dioxide through photosynthesis, they allocate a portion of the fixed carbon to mycorrhizal fungi. This carbon transfer occurs through the plant roots, providing a direct pathway for atmospheric carbon to enter the soil carbon pool.

Once in the soil, the carbon associated with mycorrhizal fungi becomes part of the stable soil organic matter, contributing to long-term carbon sequestration. This process offers a sustainable and climate-friendly mechanism for capturing atmospheric carbon and storing it in the soil, helping mitigate climate change.

The Benefits of Mycorrhizal Fungi for Climate Change Mitigation

From a climate change perspective, the association between mycorrhizal fungi and plants offers multiple advantages including:

- Nutrient exchange facilitated by mycorrhizal fungi reduces the need for synthetic fertilizers, thereby minimizing the greenhouse gas emissions associated with fertilizer production and application.

- By enhancing plant growth and yield, mycorrhizal fungi contribute to increased biomass production. This additional plant biomass acts as a sink for atmospheric carbon dioxide, promoting carbon sequestration. As the plants allocate a portion of the fixed carbon to mycorrhizal fungi, this partnership serves as an effective conduit for transferring atmospheric carbon into the soil carbon pool.

- The stable soil organic matter associated with mycorrhizal fungi helps improve soil structure and water retention, making agricultural systems more resilient to climate change impacts, such as drought and extreme weather events.

A Step-by-Step Guide:
SATURATING BIOCHAR WITH NUTRIENTS BEFORE INOCULATING WITH MYCORRHIZAL FUNGI

Materials You Will Need:

1.
BIOCHAR

2.
NUTRIENT SOLUTION

compost tea or diluted liquid organic fertilizer

3.
MYCORRHIZAL FUNGI INOCULANT

commercial product or spore solution

4.
A CONTAINER OR MIXING TOOL

5.
WATER

SATURATING BIOCHAR WITH NUTRIENTS INOCULATING WITH MYCORRHIZAL FUNGI

Step 1. | Saturate Biochar with Nutrients

Before inoculating the biochar with mycorrhizal fungi, saturate it with a nutrient solution. In a container, mix the biochar with the nutrient solution to ensure it absorbs the nutrients. Let the solution sit for a few hours or overnight to allow thorough absorption. This nutrient-enriched biochar will provide essential resources for the mycorrhizal fungi to thrive.

A Step-by-Step Guide:
SATURATING BIOCHAR WITH NUTRIENTS INOCULATING WITH MYCORRHIZAL FUNGI

Step 2. Prepare the Mycorrhizal Fungi Inoculant

Follow the instructions on the mycorrhizal fungi inoculant product for the recommended application rate. Typically, you'll need to mix a specific amount of inoculant with water to create a solution.

Step 3. Combine Biochar and Inoculant

In a container or mixing tool, combine the nutrient-saturated biochar with the mycorrhizal fungi inoculant solution. Ensure thorough mixing to evenly coat the biochar particles with the fungal spores and nutrients.

A Step-by-Step Guide:
SATURATING BIOCHAR WITH NUTRIENTS INOCULATING WITH MYCORRHIZAL FUNGI

Step 4. | Allow for Absorption

Let the biochar absorb the mycorrhizal fungi inoculant for a period specified by the product instructions. This usually takes a few hours to overnight, allowing the biochar to soak up the fungi spores and nutrients.

Step 5. | Apply to Soil

You can now apply the live biochar directly to your soil. Spread it evenly over the soil in your garden or planting area. You can mix it into the soil, add it to compost, or use it as a top dressing. The mycorrhizal fungi in the biochar will establish a symbiotic relationship with plant roots, aiding in nutrient uptake and overall plant health.

By saturating the biochar with nutrients before inoculating it with mycorrhizal fungi, you ensure that the fungi have access to essential resources, promoting a more robust and beneficial relationship with your plants.
Be sure to follow the specific instructions provided with the mycorrhizal fungi inoculant product you choose for application rates and procedures.

Chapter 3

Charging Biochar: The Power of Compost Teas

Introduction to Compost Teas for Biochar

In our quest to unlock the full potential of biochar, we explore the art of charging it with nutrient-rich compost teas. Compost teas act as a dynamic source of beneficial microorganisms, nutrients, and organic matter, augmenting the capabilities of biochar and amplifying its positive impact on soil health and plant growth.

In this chapter, we dive into the process of sustainably brewing compost teas and provide examples like using locally available organisms such as seaweed, stinging nettle, yarrow, horsetail, and even an invasive species, the rusty crayfish, to highlight the adaptability of this approach.

The Power of Compost Teas

Compost teas are created by steeping a blend of organic materials in water, allowing the beneficial microorganisms, nutrients, and other compounds to extract into the liquid. These teas serve as a concentrated source of microbial life, including bacteria, fungi, protozoa, and nematodes, that contribute to soil ecosystem resilience and plant health.

When biochar is soaked in compost tea, it becomes infused with this rich microbial diversity and nutrient content. The biochar acts as a carrier and reservoir, holding the beneficial microorganisms and slowly releasing them into the soil over time. This enhances nutrient cycling, improves soil structure, and supports plant nutrient uptake, ultimately leading to increased crop productivity.

Wildcrafting for Compost Tea Ingredients

Sustainability lies at the core of compost tea brewing. To exemplify this, let's explore the process of wildcrafting locally available ingredients for our compost tea. Stinging nettle, yarrow, and horsetail, known for their medicinal and nutritional properties, can be harvested responsibly from nearby fields, meadows, or even our own gardens.

- **Stinging Nettle** (*Urtica dioica*) - rich in nitrogen and minerals, provides a potent nutrient boost to the compost tea.

- **Yarrow** (*Achillea millefolium*) - with its beneficial essential oils, contributes to pest management and disease suppression.

- **Horsetail** (*Equisetum*) - known for its high silica content, strengthens plant cell walls, enhancing resilience against stressors.

Urtica dioica   *Achillea millefolium*   *Equisetum*

Super Seaweed!

Seaweed species have various chemical properties that make them well-suited for infusing biochar.

Seaweed species include:

- **Kelp** (*Laminaria longicruris*)
- **Rockweed** (*Fucus vesiculosus*)
- **Irish Moss** (*Chondrus crispus*)

Seaweed is rich in essential plant nutrients and trace elements that can support plant growth an development as well as contains natural plant growth hormones. These hormones can stimulate cell division, root development, and overall plant growth.

Seaweed contains:

Essentials Plant Nutrients:
- Nitrogen (N)
- Phosphorus (P)
- Potassium (K)

Trace Elements:
- Iron (Fe)
- Manganese (Mn)
- Zinc (Zn)

Plant Hormones:
- Auxins
- Cytokinins
- Gibberellins

Alginates

Seaweed also contains alginates, a compound that can improve soil structure and water-holding capacity.

Alginates help prevent the leaching of nutrients, ensuring that the plants have access to essential elements.

A Twist of Adaptability: Incorporating Rusty Crayfish

In some regions, invasive species can pose ecological challenges. Let's consider the example of the rusty crayfish—an invasive species known for its abundance in local water bodies. Rather than letting them go to waste, we can creatively incorporate the crayfish into our compost tea recipe.

By catching rusty crayfish and boiling them, we can extract valuable nutrients and minerals from their carcasses. Incorporating the boiled crayfish into the compost tea not only enriches the nutrient content but also exemplifies resourcefulness and adaptability in utilizing local resources sustainably.

Adapting the Recipe to Your Local Context

It's important to note that the rusty crayfish example provided is just one recipe using our local organisms. Every region and ecosystem has its unique array of beneficial plants, microorganisms, and organic materials that can be harnessed for compost tea brewing. By observing and engaging with the local environment, we can identify suitable ingredients and adapt the recipe accordingly.

Whether it's indigenous plants, specific compostable materials, or even invasive species, the key is to work in harmony with the local ecosystem, nurturing a sustainable and resilient approach to biochar and compost tea production.

Chapter 4

Beneficial Insects: Nature's Allies in Organic Gardening

Introduction to Beneficial Insects

Organic gardening places a strong emphasis on avoiding the use of pesticides, which necessitates finding alternative methods for managing pests effectively. In this chapter, we delve into the world of beneficial insects and explore how they can play a pivotal role in maintaining a healthy garden ecosystem. Specifically, we will focus on the process of raising beneficial nematodes in a biochar insect broth—a sustainable and natural solution to pest control that fosters soil health.

Harnessing the Power of Beneficial Nematodes

Beneficial nematodes are microscopic roundworms that offer precise pest control capabilities. These tiny organisms are effective predators of various pest species, including grubs, larvae, and other soil-dwelling pests. By integrating beneficial nematodes into our pest management strategy, we can target specific pests without harming beneficial organisms or compromising the health of the soil.

Types of Beneficial Nematodes

Heterorhabditis bacteriophora (Hb)

Steinernema feltiae (Sf)

Steinernema kraussei (Sk)

Steinernema riobrave (Sr)

Creating a Biochar Insect Broth

To raise beneficial nematodes effectively, it is recommended to utilize a biochar insect broth—a nutrient-rich liquid medium that promotes their growth and reproduction. The process begins by infusing your biochar with an insect broth derived from boiling insects like wax worms, grubs, or other insect larva.

The biochar acts as both a carrier and a source of nutrients for the nematodes. It absorbs the valuable nutrients present in the broth, creating an environment conducive to the development of beneficial nematode populations. This charged biochar becomes a reservoir of beneficial organisms that can be introduced into the garden soil.

Inoculating Biochar with Beneficial Nematodes

Once the biochar has absorbed the nutrients from the insect broth, it is time to inoculate it with beneficial nematodes. This process involves carefully introducing the nematodes onto the charged biochar, ensuring their distribution throughout the material. The biochar acts as a carrier, protecting the nematodes and facilitating their transportation into the soil.

Once in the soil, the beneficial nematodes actively seek out and infect the pest species present, effectively reducing their populations. They enter the bodies of pests, releasing bacteria that feed on the pests from within, ultimately leading to their demise. This targeted and natural method of pest control minimizes the need for chemical interventions and promotes a balanced garden ecosystem.

A Step-by-Step Guide:
RAISING ROVE BEETLES IN LARGE MASON JARS

Materials You Will Need:

1. LARGE MASON JAR

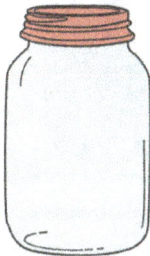

2. BIOCHAR RICH SOIL MEDIUM

3. WHOLE GRAINS

(e.g oats, barley, rice)

4. ADULT ROVE BEETLES

5. FINE MESH

or breathable fabric for covering jar

6. SMALL SPOON OR SCOOP

A Step-by-Step Guide:
RAISING ROVE BEETLES IN LARGE MASON JARS

Rove beetles are great at controlling soil pests.
It is easy to raise rove beetles in mason jars or small shoebox-sized containers using a biochar-rich soil medium, feeding them whole grains, and releasing them into your garden for effective pest control.

Step 1. Preparing the Container

Start by cleaning the mason jar to ensure there are no residues or contaminants. Fill the container with the biochar-rich soil medium, leaving about an inch of space at the top.

Step 2. Adding Rove Beetles

Order starter colony of rove beetle adults. Carefully place them into the container. Be gentle, as these insects are delicate. Cover the container with a breathable fabric or fine mesh to allow air circulation while keeping the beetles inside.

Step 3. Feeding Your Rove Beetles

Rove beetles feed on other insects and organic matter, but in a controlled environment, they can be fed whole grains. Scatter a few whole grains on the soil surface. This will serve as their food source. Monitor their food supply and add more grains when necessary. Keep the soil lightly moist, but not waterlogged.

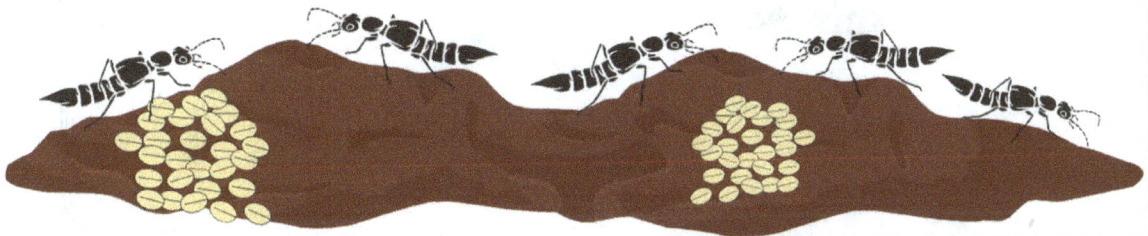

Step 4. Creating a Self-Sustaining Population

Allow the rove beetles to establish their colony. They will reproduce in the container, and their population will increase quickly. Ensure the container is kept at room temperature for optimal beetle activity.

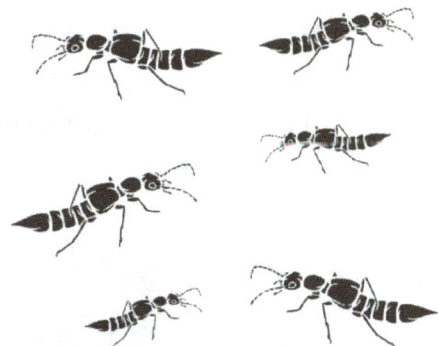

A Step-by-Step Guide:
RAISING ROVE BEETLES IN LARGE MASON JARS

Step 5. Transferring a Portion of Your Colony

When you notice that your beetle population has grown significantly and the container is approaching its capacity, it's time to transfer some of them. Carefully scoop out a portion of the beetles and biochar-rich soil and place them in a new container. Follow the same steps as in the initial setup.

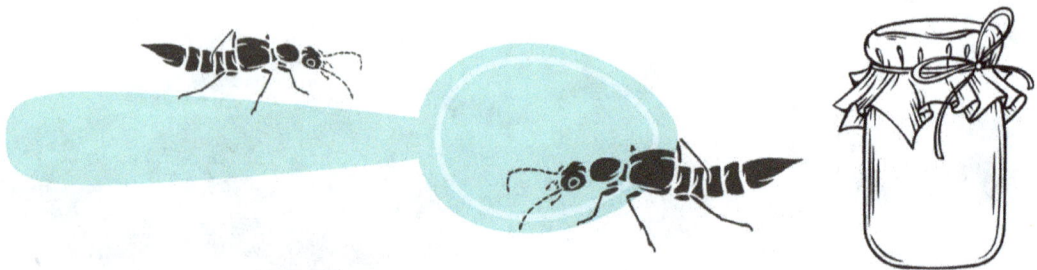

Step 6. Releasing Rove Beetles into the Garden

When you have a surplus of rove beetles in your initial container, it's time to put them to work in your garden. Simply spread the biochar-rich soil from the container, including the beetles, around your garden. This will introduce these beneficial insects to the areas where pests are a problem.

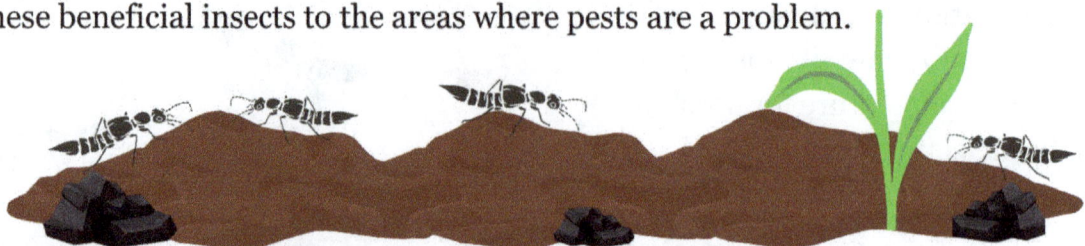

Implementing Adaptations for Local Conditions

It is important to note that the specific beneficial species and the ideal timing for their introduction may vary depending on the local conditions and target pests. Therefore, it is crucial for gardeners to research and consult local resources to determine the most suitable species for their region and the specific pests they wish to control.

Additionally, ongoing experimentation and collaboration within local gardening communities can provide valuable insights into the best practices for raising beneficial insects with biochar, allowing for continuous refinement and adaptation to local conditions.

Chapter 5

Adding Biochar to Your Garden: A Regenerative Approach

When it comes to enhancing soil health and promoting sustainable gardening practices, adding biochar to your garden can be a game-changer. In this chapter, we explore a regenerative approach that emphasizes the avoidance of tilling, the importance of preserving native mycorrhizal fungi networks, and the strategic application of compost and biochar as top dressing throughout the growing seasons. Additionally, we discuss the benefits of replenishing the soil with a layer of biochar in the fall to support the soil ecosystem after harvest.

The Pitfalls of Tilling and Soil Carbon Loss

Traditional gardening practices often involve tilling the soil, which disrupts the delicate balance of the soil ecosystem. Tilling releases stored carbon dioxide (CO_2) from the soil carbon pool, contributing to greenhouse gas emissions. Moreover, it damages the networks of native mycorrhizal fungi, which are essential for nutrient uptake and plant health.

By adopting a no-till approach, we can preserve the integrity of the soil ecosystem and minimize carbon loss, contributing to climate change mitigation while promoting soil fertility.

Strategic Application of Compost and Biochar as Top Dressing

To provide essential nutrients to plants and introduce beneficial organisms, a regenerative gardening approach involves the application of thin layers of compost and biochar as top dressing throughout the growing seasons.

Compost, rich in organic matter and nutrients, nourishes the soil and supports the growth of beneficial microorganisms. It helps improve soil structure, moisture retention, and nutrient availability to plants. By applying compost as a top dressing, we enhance the fertility of the soil and ensure a steady supply of nutrients to support plant growth.

Biochar, on the other hand, serves as a stable carbon reservoir, contributing to long-term carbon sequestration. It also provides a habitat for beneficial organisms, such as mycorrhizal fungi, which form symbiotic relationships with plant roots, aiding in nutrient uptake and promoting overall plant health.

By incorporating biochar as a top dressing, we introduce a persistent source of carbon and create a favorable environment for beneficial organisms, fostering a resilient and thriving garden ecosystem.

Replenishing the Soil with Biochar After Harvest

In the fall, after the harvest season, it is crucial to replenish the soil and prepare it for the following growing season. A highly effective approach is to apply a thick layer of nutrient-rich biochar as a top dressing.

This thick layer of biochar acts as a protective blanket for the soil, providing numerous benefits. It helps retain moisture, and creates a favorable habitat for beneficial organisms during the dormant winter months.

Adapting the Approach to Your Garden's Needs

It is important to note that every garden is unique, and the specific application of compost and biochar will depend on various factors such as soil type, climate, and plant requirements. Observation and experimentation are key to understanding the needs of your garden and adapting the regenerative approach accordingly.

By monitoring plant health, soil moisture, and nutrient levels, gardeners can fine-tune the application of compost and biochar, ensuring optimal results for their specific garden ecosystem.

Chapter 6

Get Involved!

Encourage your local and federal government to make biochar production a key tool in the fight against climate change!

Hobby gardeners, professional horticulturalists, and farmers who understand the potential of biochar have already started harnessing its benefits to improve soil health and sequester vast amounts of carbon. While individual efforts are admirable, it's also important to take our commitment to the next level. It's vital to engage with our local and federal governments to make biochar production a key tool in the battle against climate change.

As individuals, we can make a significant impact by using biochar in our gardens and farms. The reality is that our capacity to make a real difference in the battle against climate change is radically multiplied when we engage with our government.

Local and federal governments have the power to implement large-scale biochar production and application strategies that can yield dramatic results.

Consider this, if your local government were to convert green waste from your city into biochar, it would not only reduce waste but also sequester carbon effectively.

Similarly, asking your federal government to mitigate the damage caused by the invasive insects devastating our forests by converting infested trees into biochar is a force multiplier in the fight against climate change.

These actions on a governmental scale can sequester carbon and restore ecosystems at a rate that is unattainable through individual efforts alone.

While every individual's efforts to sequester carbon in their own soil are commendable, it's time to magnify our impact by engaging with our government. The scale at which governments operate makes them pivotal players in the fight against climate change. By encouraging your government to invest in biochar production and application, you can be part of the solution to one of the most pressing challenges of our time.

Let's unite our voices and turn biochar into a powerful force against climate change. Together, we can create a more sustainable and resilient future for our planet.

Facebook.com/CarbonInTheGarden

@carbon.in.the.garden

Further Reading

Ayaz, M.; Feizienė, D.; Tilvikienė, V.; Akhtar, K.; Stulpinaitė, U.; Iqbal, R. Biochar Role in the Sustainability of Agriculture and Environment. Sustainability 2021, 13, 1330. https://doi.org/10.3390/su13031330

Das, S.K., Ghosh, G.K. & Avasthe, R. Application of biochar in agriculture and environment, and its safety issues. Biomass Conv. Bioref. 13, 1359–1369 (2023). https://doi.org/10.1007/s13399-020-01013-4

Hua, L., Lu, Z., Ma, H., & Jin, S. (2014). Effect of biochar on carbon dioxide release, organic carbon accumulation, and aggregation of soil. Environmental Progress & Sustainable Energy, 33(3), 941-946. https://doi.org/10.1002/ep.11867

Jha, Pramod, et al. "Biochar in Agriculture – Prospects and Related Implications." Current Science, vol. 99, no. 9, 2010, pp. 1218–25. JSTOR, http://www.jstor.org/stable/24068517.

Joseph, S., Cowie, A. L., Zwieten, L. V., Bolan, N., Budai, A., Buss, W., Cayuela, M. L., Graber, E. R., Ippolito, J. A., Kuzyakov, Y., Luo, Y., Ok, Y. S., Palansooriya, K. N., Shepherd, J., Stephens, S., & Lehmann, J. (2021). How biochar works, and when it doesn't: A review of mechanisms controlling soil and plant responses to biochar. GCB Bioenergy, 13(11), 1731-1764. https://doi.org/10.1111/gcbb.12885

Li, H., Yutong, W., Tianpei, W., & Hongrui, M. (2015). Effect of biochar on organic matter conservation and metabolic quotient of soil. Environmental Progress & Sustainable Energy, 34(5), 1467-1472. https://doi.org/10.1002/ep.12122

Liu, S., Zhang, Y., Zong, Y., Hu, Z., Wu, S., Zhou, J., Jin, Y., & Zou, J. (2016). Response of soil carbon dioxide fluxes, soil organic carbon and microbial biomass carbon to biochar amendment: A meta-analysis. GCB Bioenergy, 8(2), 392-406. https://doi.org/10.1111/gcbb.12265

Longlong Xia, Wenhao Chen, Bufan Lu, Shanshan Wang,et al. Climate mitigation potential of sustainable biochar production in China, Renewable and Sustainable Energy Reviews, Volume 175, 2023, 113145, ISSN 1364-0321, https://doi.org/10.1016/j.rser.2023.113145.(https://www.sciencedirect.com/science/article/pii/S1364032123000011)

Lorenz, K., & Lal, R. (2014). Biochar application to soil for climate change mitigation by soil organic carbon sequestration. Journal of Plant Nutrition and Soil Science, 177(5), 651-670. https://doi.org/10.1002/jpln.201400058

Quilliam, R. S., Glanville, H. C., Wade, S. C., & Jones, D. L. (2013). Life in the 'charosphere' – Does biochar in agricultural soil provide a significant habitat for microorganisms? Soil Biology and Biochemistry, 65, 287-293. https://doi.org/10.1016/j.soilbio.2013.06.004

Schmidt, P., Kammann, C., Hagemann, N., Leifeld, J., Bucheli, T. D., Sánchez Monedero, M. A., & Cayuela, M. L. (2021). Biochar in agriculture – A systematic review of 26 global meta-analyses. GCB Bioenergy, 13(11), 1708-1730. https://doi.org/10.1111/gcbb.12889

Xia, L., Chen, W., Lu, B., Wang, S., Xiao, L., Liu, B., Yang, H., Huang, C., Wang, H., Yang, Y., Lin, L., Zhu, X., Chen, W., Yan, X., Zhuang, M., Kung, C., Zhu, Y., & Yang, Y. (2023). Climate mitigation potential of sustainable biochar production in China. Renewable and Sustainable Energy Reviews, 175, 113145. https://doi.org/10.1016/j.rser.2023.113145

Yu, Y., Harper, M., Hoepfl, M., & Domermuth, D. (2017). Characterization of biochar and its effects on the water holding capacity of loamy sand soil: Comparison of hemlock biochar and switchblade grass biochar characteristics. Environmental Progress & Sustainable Energy, 36(5), 1474-1479. https://doi.org/10.1002/ep.12592

CARBON in the GARDEN

ORGANIC TIPS FOR A SUSTAINABLE GARDEN AND PLANET

Emily Morris   Nathaniel Morris

www.ingramcontent.com/pod-product-compliance
Lightning Source LLC
Chambersburg PA
CBHW081521040426
42447CB00013B/3288